MAY 1 6 2016

TURNING POINTS IN US HISTORY

12 INCREDIBLE FACTS ABOUT THE
LOUISIANA PURCHASE

by Anita Yasuda

12 STORY LIBRARY

www.12StoryLibrary.com

12-Story Library is an imprint of Peterson Publishing Company and Press Room Editions.

Produced for 12-Story Library by Red Line Editorial

Photographs ©: Bettmann/Corbis/AP Images, cover, 1, 6, 10, 20, 23, 28, 29; Henry R. Robinson/Library of Congress, 4; gavni/iStockphoto/Red Line Editorial, 5; Goupil & Cie/ Library of Congress, 7; Library of Congress, 8, 15, 21, 24; North Wind Picture Archives, 9; Gianni Dagli Orti/Corbis, 11; Linda Steward/iStockphoto, 12; Bettmann/Corbis, 13, 16, 18; Gilbert Stuart/Detroit Publishing Company/Library of Congress, 14; Corbis, 17; duncan1890/ iStockphoto, 19; JanvdBrink/iStockphoto, 22; Thomas Arbour/iStockphoto, 25; George A. Crofutt/Library of Congress, 26; traveler1116/iStockphoto, 27

ISBN
978-1-63235-131-9 (hardcover)
978-1-63235-174-6 (paperback)
978-1-62143-226-5 (hosted ebook)

Library of Congress Control Number: 2015933985

Printed in the United States of America
Mankato, MN
June, 2015

Go beyond the book. Get free, up-to-date content on this topic at 12StoryLibrary.com.

TABLE OF CONTENTS

JEFFERSON DREAMS OF AN "EMPIRE OF LIBERTY"

At the beginning of the 1800s, the United States did not look like it does today. It was much smaller. Most Americans lived on the East Coast, near the Atlantic Ocean.

There were only 16 states. Great Britain held the land to the north. Spain controlled the Floridas to the South and the land in the far west. The Floridas included the present-day Florida and the land along the coast of Louisiana. France claimed the central part of what is the United States today.

In 1801, Thomas Jefferson became the third president of the United States. Since he was a young boy, Jefferson had been fascinated with the West. But no one knew much about the geography or wildlife of the area. Even less was known about

President Thomas Jefferson

DISTRICT OF MAINE
VERMONT
NEW HAMPSHIRE
MASSACHUSETTS
NEW YORK
RHODE ISLAND
CONNECTICUT
PENNSYLVANIA
NEW JERSEY
DELAWARE
MARYLAND
VIRGINIA
KENTUCKY
NORTH CAROLINA
TENNESSEE
SOUTH CAROLINA
GEORGIA
MISSISSIPPI TERRITORY
SPANISH FLORIDA
INDIANA TERRITORY
OHIO
LOUISIANA TERRITORY
BRITISH TERRITORY
SPANISH TERRITORY
MISSISSIPPI RIVER
PACIFIC OCEAN
ATLANTIC OCEAN
GULF OF MEXICO

N W E S

North America in 1803

the hundreds of American Indian tribes living there.

The West was part of Jefferson's dream of an "empire of liberty." He believed that the United States needed to grow. Before the end of his first term, Jefferson would have the opportunity to buy land from the Mississippi River all the way to the Rocky Mountains. This area was called Louisiana Territory.

8

Number of years Thomas Jefferson served as president.

- Jefferson wanted the United States to grow.
- Jefferson wanted the West explored.
- In the early 1800s, parts of the present-day United States were owned by Great Britain, Spain, and France.
- Many American Indian tribes lived in the West.

LOUIS XIV CALLS LOUISIANA "QUITE USELESS!"

On April 9, 1682, French explorer René-Robert Cavelier de La Salle reached the mouth of the Mississippi River. La Salle claimed the land west of the Mississippi for France, even though American Indian tribes had been living there for centuries. He named the land Louisiana, after the King of France, Louis XIV. But the king wasn't impressed. He called the discovery "quite useless!"

It wasn't until 1699 that the French set up a colony in the territory. Settlers from France and Germany came to live there. They cleared the land and built farms. Not long after, French-speakers from Canada moved there too. Later, people in Africa and the West Indies, a group of islands in the Caribbean Sea, were captured and brought in to work the land as slaves.

In 1754, fighting began between Great Britain and France. It is known as the French and Indian War (1754–1763). During the war, France gave up Louisiana to its ally, Spain. Under Spanish control, commerce in Louisiana grew.

René-Robert Cavelier de La Salle

Meanwhile, by the late 1700s, more Americans began to settle the lands between the Appalachian Mountains and the Mississippi River.

Louis XIV didn't think Louisiana was worth much.

64
Number of years Louisiana was a French colony.

- Louisiana Territory was named for King Louis XIV.
- The French built the first settlement there in 1699.
- Trade in Louisiana grew under the Spanish.
- American settlers began to move farther west.

NATCHEZ TRIBE

For hundreds of years, American Indian tribes have lived west of the Mississippi River. One of these tribes is the Natchez. From the early 1700s, French colonialists began to build farms on their homelands. Angered, the Natchez Indians attacked the French. French troops put down the attack. The Natchez were defeated.

NEW ORLEANS PORT CLOSING STARTS WITH A RUMOR

On October 27, 1795, the United States signed a treaty with Spain. It gave Americans the right to use the Mississippi River for trade. The United States was also granted the right of deposit. This meant Americans could store goods in New Orleans before they were shipped elsewhere. The treaty encouraged more Americans to move to Louisiana to take advantage of the trade.

Then, in 1800, a rumor spread of a secret deal between France and Spain. The deal, if true, gave Louisiana back to France. France was ruled by Napoleon Bonaparte. He wanted to create a new French empire in North America. Louisiana was an important part of his plan. He thought the land could be used to grow food for French troops in the West Indies.

Although no one in the United States knew it yet, the rumor was true. On October 1, 1800, Napoleon had signed the Treaty of San Ildefonso with Spain. This gave Louisiana Territory back to France.

Napoleon Bonaparte hoped to use Louisiana to grow food for French troops.

Western settlers worried that the port of New Orleans would be closed.

American settlers in the West were worried. They wondered if France might close the port of New Orleans. If it did, they would not be able to move or sell their goods. Jefferson needed to find out if the rumor was true.

1799
Year Napoleon Bonaparte became first consul, France's political leader.

- France acquired Louisiana on October 1, 1800, from Spain.
- Napoleon wanted to re-establish a French empire in North America.
- Jefferson worried that merchant ships would not be able to use New Orleans port.

AN IMPORTANT PORT

Settlers sold off extra products, such as grain, to merchants. It was not easy to move heavy cargo over the Appalachian Mountains to the East Coast. The Ohio River and Mississippi River were an easier way to ship goods to the busy port of New Orleans. From there, goods were sent to Europe or the Northeast.

ROBERT LIVINGSTON FACES STALEMATE IN FRANCE

Robert Livingston was an experienced politician. He was known as a good negotiator. Jefferson needed a man with these skills. In 1801, he sent Livingston to France. The president asked him to find out if France was taking back New Orleans from Spain. If true, Livingston was to offer France money

> Robert Livingston was sent to France to negotiate.

RULER OF FRANCE

Napoleon Bonaparte rose to power during the French Revolution. He was a skilled military leader who won many battles. In 1799, he used his success in battle to become the ruler of France. Five years later, he named himself Emperor of France.

for New Orleans and the Floridas.

However, Livingston's patience would be tested in France. For almost two years he met with French officials. Napoleon's minister of foreign affairs, Charles Maurice de Talleyrand dodged his questions. Talleyrand was a wily politician. He denied that Spain and France had signed a treaty.

It was a very frustrating time for Livingston. There was no French legislature. Napoleon ruled over everything. He didn't often ask his ministers for advice when he made decisions. They had no real power.

Livingston wrote essays and letters to French officials. In them, he explained why the French should sell Louisiana. It would be a poor market for French goods, he wrote. Still, Livingston had no luck. Napoleon was not willing to sell Louisiana.

Talleyrand dealt with foreign affairs for Napoleon.

14

Number of months Robert Livingston spent negotiating with the French.

- Livingston left for France in 1801.
- Livingston negotiated with French officials, attempting to purchase New Orleans and the Floridas.
- France refused to sell.
- Napoleon Bonaparte held all the power in France.

NEW ORLEANS IS CLOSED

Once Jefferson learned France owned New Orleans, he was alarmed. On October 16, 1802, his worry turned to anger. The Spanish colonial administrator posted a notice. As part of the sale to France, the Spanish closed the port of New Orleans to Americans.

This created a huge problem for farmers along the Mississippi River. They had goods such as flour and meat to get to market. In 1802 alone, over $1.5 million in goods were exported through the Mississippi. The farmers were angry. Some demanded war with France to regain the port. They saw this as a violation of the 1795 treaty with Spain. They wanted their government to act at once.

Jefferson realized that the young nation's economy was at risk. The United States appealed to Spain,

New Orleans had been an important port for Americans.

Napoleon with his family and associates

1/2

Amount of the United States' food supply that was being grown in the West.

- Spain closed New Orleans to US ships.
- Closing the port created a problem for farmers in the West who needed to ship their goods.
- Americans wanted their government to act.

explaining that access to the Mississippi River was crucial to American trade. But they'd have to deal with the French.

THINK ABOUT IT

How did closing the port of New Orleans affect Americans? Find evidence from these pages to support your answer.

NAPOLEON NEEDS MONEY

Jefferson sent James Monroe to help Livingston in France. By the time Monroe arrived in Paris, the situation had changed. The French were now offering to sell all of Louisiana. Livingston and Monroe were surprised.

Napoleon had been forced to change his mind. In 1803, Great Britain and France were not on friendly terms. It looked as if the two countries would soon go to war. Napoleon needed money for this war. He hoped he could get it by selling Louisiana.

Also, Napoleon had sent 30,000 French troops to put down an uprising in its colony Saint-Domingue in the West Indies. Much to his surprise the troops failed. Yellow fever, a tropical disease, killed most of the French army there. Napoleon could not afford to send troops to North America if a conflict started there too.

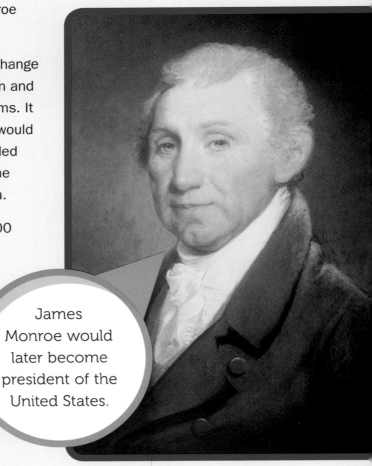

James Monroe would later become president of the United States.

Enslaved people in Saint-Domingue fought against French troops.

Napoleon told his financial minister, François Barbé-Marbois, to ask 50 million francs ($11,250,000) for Louisiana. And Napoleon wanted the territory sold fast. The minister, wanting to please Napoleon, doubled the asking price.

3,000
Number of French soldiers who died in less than one month at the beginning of the yellow fever epidemic.

- French troops in Saint-Domingue suffered from a yellow fever epidemic.
- Napoleon needed more money for a war with Great Britain.
- Napoleon decided to sell Louisiana.

UNITED STATES BUYS LOUISIANA TERRITORY

Monroe and Livingston believed that Jefferson would want Louisiana. But Congress had only authorized $2 million for the sale. The French wanted more than ten times that amount. Before Monroe left for France, Jefferson told him that they could offer up to $10 million for just New Orleans and the Floridas.

It took months for letters to reach the United States. So Monroe and Livingston acted alone. They did not want to risk losing the deal. They wanted to close it before Napoleon changed his mind. The two men worked to negotiate a lower price.

Finally, on April 30, 1803, the two sides agreed to $15 million. They signed the treaty on May 2, 1803. It became known as the Louisiana Purchase. Under the treaty, the United States added 828,000 square miles (2,144,520 sq km) to its land. That worked out to less than 5 cents per acre.

Jefferson didn't learn of the deal until July 3. He didn't believe that the US Constitution gave him power to buy the land. But he agreed with Monroe's and Livingston's decision to act. Waiting for Congress's approval might have taken too long.

From left to right, Barbé-Marbois, Livingston, and Monroe sign the Louisiana Purchase.

Treaty

Between the United States of America

and the French Republic

The President of the United States of America
Consul of the French Republic in the name of
People desiring to remove all Source of misunde

Jefferson hoped that Americans would agree with his decision. On July 4, 1803, Jefferson announced the deal to the public. Most Americans were excited. The United States had doubled in size. The future was full of opportunity for the young country. Congress eventually approved the purchase in October 1803.

OPPOSITION TO THE DEAL

Some members of Congress disagreed with the deal. They thought it was unconstitutional. After all, it had been made without the consent of the Senate. One paper in Boston wondered why the government was giving away money which the country had little of, for land it already had so much of.

5

Approximate number of months between the signing of the Louisiana Purchase in France and Congress's approval of the deal.

- Louisiana Territory cost $15 million.
- The purchase doubled the size of the country.
- The United States paid less than 5 cents per acre of land.

JEFFERSON WANTS THE WEST EXPLORED

On December 20, 1803, the flag of the United States was raised in New Orleans. The United States officially owned all of Louisiana. However, the area was largely unknown except to American Indian tribes. Many Americans wondered what the United States had actually bought. Even Louisiana's boundaries were not defined.

At the time, there were many stories about the West. There was talk of a great mountain of salt. Some people believed there were unicorns and woolly mammoths. Jefferson decided it was time to know what lay out west. In fact, he began planning the

NORTHWEST PASSAGE

It took traders a long time to sail from Europe to Asia. Ships either had to travel around the tip of Africa or South America. For this reason, people wanted to find a passage through North America. This undiscovered route was called the Northwest Passage.

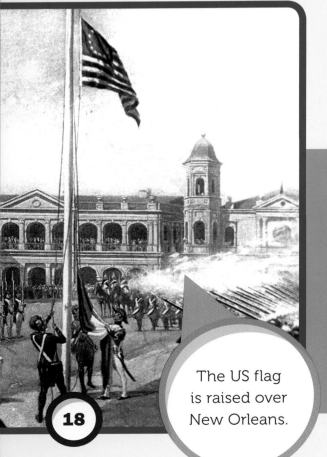

The US flag is raised over New Orleans.

$2,500

Amount Jefferson requested from Congress to fund the journey.

- At the time of purchase, little was known about Louisiana Territory.
- People thought woolly mammoths and unicorns might live in the West.
- Jefferson thought exploring the West might open up new trading opportunities.

money to explore the region. He wanted to learn more about western plant and animal life. He wanted to open trade with western American Indian tribes. The president also hoped explorers would find a water route to the Pacific Ocean. This would mean an easier way for goods to travel across North America to Asia.

trip long before the deal with France was even signed.

In January 1803, Jefferson had sent a letter to Congress asking for

Woolly mammoth bones had been found in the eastern part of the country, so people wondered if they might find live mammoths in the West.

JEFFERSON SELECTS SECRETARY TO LEAD EXPEDITION

Once Jefferson received funding from Congress, an expedition to explore the West could go ahead.

But who would head this trip? Jefferson didn't have to look far. He chose his secretary, Meriwether Lewis. Lewis chose his friend William Clark to help him. They had met while serving in the US Army.

Before the team left, Jefferson carefully planned the trip. The president's library held more books about the West than any other library in the world. The president studied letters, reports, and maps by people who had been to Louisiana. He put together notes on the geography, people, and resources of the region.

In the meantime, Lewis needed to learn new skills before he set off. He went to Philadelphia for a month to meet with scientists. He learned about map making, fossils,

Lewis picked his friend William Clark as his partner for the trip.

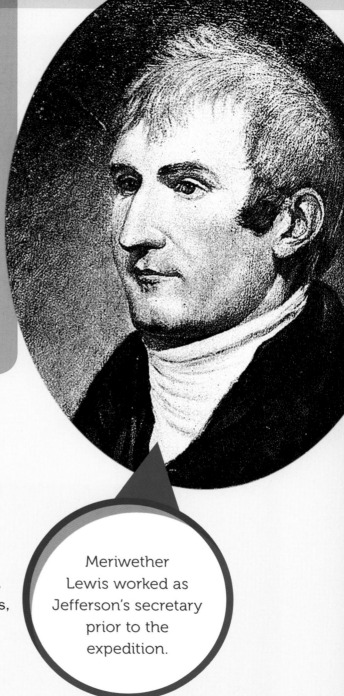

33

Approximate number of people in the expedition team when it began.

- Meriwether Lewis headed the expedition.
- Lewis hired William Clark as a partner.
- Jefferson provided the team with research about the West.
- Lewis learned about map making, fossils, and botany to prepare for the trip.

and botany. He studied navigation and how to preserve animals and plant samples.

Lewis also had to buy everything the team might need on the trip. He collected two tons (1.8 t) worth of supplies. They included a microscope and a compass. There were also camping supplies, presents for American Indian tribes, extra clothing, and medicine.

Meriwether Lewis worked as Jefferson's secretary prior to the expedition.

LEWIS AND CLARK CHART UNKNOWN TERRITORY

On May 4, 1804, the Lewis and Clark Expedition team, called the Corps of Discovery, set out from St. Louis, Missouri, to explore the West. It was an exciting time. No one knew what they would find. Over the next few months, the group paddled and portaged up the Missouri River to Fort Mandan. The fort is in today's central North Dakota. They waited out the winter there. They sent samples to the president by boat, including a curious whistling squirrel. It was a prairie dog.

At the beginning of April 1805, the team left for the Pacific coast. Two new members of the group joined them. They were interpreter and guide Toussaint Charbonneau and his wife, Sacagawea, who was part of the Shoshone tribe. Sacagawea became an important member of

Lewis and Clark sent a live prairie dog back to the president.

4

Number of months the group spent at Fort Mandan.

- The journey began May 4, 1804, in St. Louis, Missouri.
- Sacagawea played an important role.
- The team reached the Pacific Ocean in mid-November.

THINK ABOUT IT

If you had been a member of the expedition, what would you have hoped to find out? Explain your choice.

the group. She helped them find food. She secured horses from the Shoshone.

The team traveled for thousands of miles along rivers. They climbed mountains covered with snow and ice. They carved their own canoes and made their own clothes. They met and traded with many American Indian tribes along the way. Then, one day in November 1805, they heard the thundering sound of the ocean. The team was filled with joy. Finally, they had made it to the Pacific Ocean. They were the first Americans to reach the Pacific by land.

Sacagawea helped guide the expedition.

EXPLORERS BELIEVED DEAD BEFORE RETURN

The Corps of Discovery team hoped a ship would take them home once they reached the Pacific Ocean. But it never arrived. They had to spend the winter of 1805 on the coast. On the long trip back east, they battled strong rivers and fierce storms. When snow hid the route through the Bitterroot Mountains, members of the Nez Perce tribe helped them find their way. Once over this hurdle, Lewis and Clark separated in early July. They wanted to investigate more of Louisiana. The two groups reunited on the Missouri River on August 12.

On September 23, 1806, the team arrived home in St. Louis. Their journey had taken them two years, four months, and ten days. More

An 1810 illustration showed Lewis and Clark meeting with American Indians during the expedition.

than 1,000 people came out to welcome them back. Many, including Jefferson, thought the men were lost or dead.

The team reported their incredible findings to Jefferson. Their journals were filled with information on American Indian tribes they had met. They recorded more than 300 species, including at least 150 mammals. Lewis and Clark were the first explorers to describe grizzly bears and bighorn sheep. Clark made several maps showing major landforms such as the Rocky Mountains. He charted the course of the Missouri River and other major rivers. These maps would be valuable to later explorers.

55

Number of American Indian tribes Lewis and Clark met on their journey.

- The team spent the winter of 1805 on the West Coast.
- They arrived back in St. Louis on September 23, 1806.
- The return journey took 249 days.

Lewis and Clark saw the Rocky Mountains and other land formations during their expedition.

12

LOUISIANA PURCHASE CHANGES AMERICA

Lewis and Clark's experiences in the West excited people. The West seemed like an amazing place. People heard that there were lots of animals to trap and fish to catch. There were many other natural resources too, such as timber. Later, gold and other minerals would be found there too. Americans eager for land and these

In this painting, a woman symbolizes the idea of "manifest destiny," as settlers follow her west and American Indians and bison run away.

resources began to move to the West.

However, this region was already home to many American Indian tribes. They had farmed, trapped, and hunted on this land long before American explorers came. But most Americans didn't think these tribes had any rights to the land.

In the 1830s, the idea of "manifest destiny" became popular. Americans believed that it was their right to extend the country all the way to the West Coast. Some saw it as God's will.

The US government took the land from American Indian tribes. They gave it to white settlers. Eventually, American Indians were forced onto reservations. Others were killed by the government and settlers.

Thousands of settlers made their way west. The journey was difficult but these people were determined to start new lives. Within 100 years, parts of 15 states would be created from the Louisiana Purchase.

A 2004 postage stamp celebrated Lewis and Clark's journey.

15
Number of states created from the Louisiana Purchase.

- After Lewis and Clark's expedition, people were excited about the West.
- The new land was rich with natural resources.
- Many Americans saw it as their right and duty to expand into the West.
- Westward expansion devastated American Indian tribes.

12 KEY DATES

April 9, 1682
Robert Cavelier de La Salle, a French adventurer, claims Louisiana Territory for Louis XIV.

October 27, 1795
The United States signs a treaty with Spain allowing Americans to store goods in New Orleans without paying tax.

October 1, 1800
Napoleon Bonaparte, ruler of France, signs the Treaty of San Ildefonso with Spain, reclaiming Louisiana Territory.

December 1801
Robert Livingston arrives in Paris to negotiate.

October 16, 1802
Spain closes the port of New Orleans and withdraws American right of deposit.

April 30, 1803
Representatives from France and the United States sign the Louisiana Purchase treaty.

July 4, 1803
Jefferson announces the purchase of Louisiana.

October 1803
Congress approves the Louisiana Purchase.

May 4, 1804
The Corps of Discovery leaves St. Louis to explore Louisiana Territory.

April 1805
The Corps leaves Fort Mandan, continuing west.

November 1805
The Corps reaches the Pacific Ocean.

September 23, 1806
After a journey which took over two years, the Corps arrives back in St. Louis, Missouri.

GLOSSARY

botany
The study of plants.

commerce
When goods or services are exchanged for money.

economy
The system of making and using goods and services.

empire
When a political power controls a huge territory.

legislature
The part of a government that makes laws.

mouth
The part of a river that flows to a lake, ocean, or other body of water.

negotiate
A discussion aimed at reaching an agreement.

portage
To carry a boat from one waterway to another or around an obstacle such as a waterfall.

reservations
Areas of land reserved for American Indians to use.

territory
An area owned by a country or government.

treaty
An agreement between two or more groups usually to end a conflict.

FOR MORE INFORMATION

Books

Benoit, Peter. *The Louisiana Purchase*. New York: Scholastic, 2012.

Landau, Elaine. *The Louisiana Purchase: Would You Close the Deal?* New York: Enslow Publishers, 2010.

Sanford, William R. and Carl R. Green. *Sacagawea: Courageous American Indian Guide.* New York: Enslow Publishers, 2013.

St. George, Judith. *What Was the Lewis and Clark Expedition?* New York: Grosset and Dunlap, 2014.

Websites

The Journals of the Lewis and Clark Expedition
lewisandclarkjournals.unl.edu

National Geographic: Lewis and Clark
www.nationalgeographic.com/lewisandclark

PBS: Lewis and Clark
www.pbs.org/lewisandclark

INDEX

About the Author

Anita Yasuda is the author of more than 100 books for children. She enjoys writing biographies, books about science and social studies, and chapter books. Anita lives with her family in California.